T0146852

In Retrospect

FORESIGHT, HINDSIGHT, AND AT TIMES NO SIGHT AT ALL

A book of Lyrics and Lyric Poetry
Written and compiled by:

Michael F. Domaracki

authorHOUSE®

AuthorHouse™
1663 Liberty Drive
Bloomington, IN 47403
www.authorhouse.com
Phone: 1 (800) 839-8640

Published by AuthorHouse   10/09/2015

ISBN: 978-1-5049-4868-5 (sc)
ISBN: 978-1-5049-4869-2 (e)

Library of Congress Control Number: 2015914448

Print information available on the last page.

Any people depicted in stock imagery provided by Thinkstock are models, and such images are being used for illustrative purposes only. Certain stock imagery © Thinkstock.

This book is printed on acid-free paper.

Acknowledgements...

I want to thank my wife, Adrianne for being the true catalyst behind this book becoming a realization. Her endless support and encouragement over the years and especially in more recent months has been a source of inspiration that I cannot fully explain. I love you, my dearest Adrianne. Also, to our children Brenden and Erin, now young adults, who fully understand the importance of doing something you love and the happiness that comes along with it. You both have done your Mom and I proud. To the select few others that have been privy to some of my writing, both contained here and as of yet unpublished pieces. Your interest in my interests, along with your support has long had a positive impact on my continued writing. To the Poetry Soup community for embracing the works not only of mine, but of everyone of the thousands of writers, poets, lyricists and other aspiring, accomplished, and successful writers who access the Poetry Soup website to share their lives and emotions via the written word.

Introduction...

So here we begin to tell the tale. Snapshots of various moments throughout my life, now out there to be shared with whomever may feel inclined to go there, to go along for the ride, so to speak. I believe that much of what is contained here is relatable to nearly everyone at one point or another in their lives. It is my hope that anyone reading through these verses will find something they can grab onto, that will resound with them some feeling or emotion that they, themselves have felt or have been feeling. Though there is a certain vagueness of meaning in some of the writing here, so too does that allow for various interpretations based on the individual reading through the verses, allowing for a much wider range of emotion to be encompassed. I began writing years ago as a way of verbalizing so many of the things that, being a quiet person by nature, I would never speak aloud. This current collection of lyrics, lyric poetry, or simply poetry if you would rather call it has been compiled from many years of writing, from a time when the only way to capture it was to sit and put pen or pencil to paper (which was not really that long ago), up through the current time when it could be typed on the go via computer, tablet, etc...At any rate, the story does indeed begin here. However, it is only the beginning...

Michael Domaracki

My idols are the authors, whose pages I slowly turn
And the musicians, for theirs is the
stage for which I yearn...

On Paper...

Marching through time
Losing track of it all
How fast time flies
When you're feeling good
Having fun without a care
Now all of your concern is real
Running scared of situations in your life
And your feelings…

You don't know what to do with yourself
You are never alone
The chance to sit
And think your thoughts on paper
Before you lose your mind
Or the idea inside your head
I have got to get it out,
Get it down on paper for myself

Here I go again, fighting to find the time
Ignoring certain situations, in order to rhyme these words
Stories, bits and pieces of my life, I have locked away
Saved for a rainy day, when you cannot find the feeling
And you are looking on paper for solutions…

Into the Light of the Day...

Front from back who can tell how many lives are changing
Beginning to end
We start and finish time and again
Enter and exit, we come and go but no one knows
Just what it all means to me

Doors unlocked remain unopened for lack of challenge
I only cross where others would not dare look back on
I find intensity in the fight to carry on
Survive for you and I, you and I…

Unfinished works lie untouched in the process
But at hand we have created another chapter,
This verse
And tomorrow, saving me from today
Will find this pen in hand
Guiding myself and any believers
Out of the darkness of the forest
And into the light of the day…

The Gallery...

Another day goes by, outside influence on the outcome
Tearing the heartstring in two
And in my mind strange topics pop up again
Without your love in my life, I don't know what I would do
On the home front, on my own
It seems I'm alone, to pick up all of the little pieces
Build a picture perfect puzzle out of nothing
But four walls as a frame that I am supposed to hang…

Trying to change my life, while my world changes around me
Mixed priorities linger in my mind
Live for myself, live for everybody else
Constant turmoil as we pass through time together
Depth of thought for me serves as prayer
To our God, or my God in my eyes
I seldom ask for more than reasons why things happen
To understand and to know he hears my cries…

Snapshots in a photo album, memories in my mind
Like episodes in syndication over and over again
A constant circle of events repeating through my life
Were the lessons ever learned or does the lesson never end…?
Look, gaze into the four walls at how much lies inside, see how much things have to change
Hanging on the walls are scars left from all of the pain
And though I try to put it in the past, most of it remains, in the Gallery…

One by One...

Concrete words cement my fears, one by one commit to line
Carved in stone all through the years
A labor of love and time
A lesson to learn that nothing good will come
To those who cannot wait
A patient man whose concrete words
Serve to document his fate
And one by one they're commit to line
One by one with love, through time…

I can't help but keep coming back to that which brought me here
A mere mortal man who finally learned how to keep his conscience clear
A lesson learned that nothing good will come to those who cannot wait
A blessed man is he whose love can survive in all this hate
And through darkened days still hold the line…
Balanced on the straight and narrow

Concrete words cement my fears, one by one commit to line
Carved in stone all through the years
So some good would come in time…
One by one, a labor of love and time
One word, one day, each in its own time…

Concrete words cement my fears, one by one commit to line
Realizing just how clear it is, this is only part of the design…
Better times will soon arrive…believe

Behind These Eyes...

Behind these eyes
What evil lurks,
What beauty skirts the edges of my mind?
Hand in hand with such subtlety
And gale force wind
Trapped for just one moment in time

Capture the moment
Freeze frame on the screen
Photographed in still life
And yet it's fading like a dream
Time draws its own conclusions
Not much matters for you or I
Good intent has always led to hell
Truth nothing more than a well wrapped lie

Behind these eyes
What evil lurks,
What beauty skirts the edges of my mind?
Hand in hand with such subtlety
And gale force wind
I'm trapped within the eye of this storm…

All on Me...

I can't help but feel the strain of the weight of a world I created
Can't mistake my inner faults and guilt that I have fallen way to short
No serenade can I sing to you and of that I am ashamed
No resolution and no compromise on the position I am in
No other answer to the question than to turn and look at me
Point the finger in my direction because in the end it is all on me...

Can I right the wrongs that I've done each day
Can two wrongs make a right of me
Can I face the failures of my past or of this day right here and now
If the mirror reflects the shadow or the light, and if I remain a part of the
picture we'll see
I am short on definition but long on words that paint the picture
Feeling like I can't move from day to day...

I believe I must align my heart and mind as one
My body and my soul right behind
They must follow suit they must fall into line
It may be my last chance at life.....and it's high time we stood to live....

No resolution and no compromise I cannot sacrifice our needs, in the end
it is all on me
No other answer to the question than to turn and look at me
Point the finger in my direction because in the end it is all on me....
For how long will you believe this dream??
I want it all to fall on me...

Mortal Man...

I've awakened all my demons and it suddenly appears
The death of all my dreams and the re-birth of all of my fears
Times I know I'm not alone, other times, like now I know I am
Sinking down just like a stone, no strength for my last stand
See me...breaking down
See me...a mere mortal man
There's certain sadness that courses through my veins
A delicate and fine line to manage all my pain
Some of it imagined, how much of it is real
The only gauge I have is the way that I now feel

See me...breaking down, king without his crown
A mere mortal man, whose life slipped through his hands
See me...breaking down, blood spilled on the ground
A mere mortal man, this is not what he had planned

Our world a tainted paradise, in which everyone must live
Always for the chosen few, the rest of us must give
No reciprocation as good intent declines
Even outcast by our families, for those we did provide
Expendable, disposable...yes, each of us must die
But how many of us have truly lived, and not been forced to live a lie

See me...breaking down, never a king that wore a crown
A mere mortal man, and this is not what he had planned...

Powerless (Dark Clichés)...

In a rage, in disarray, I can't help but feel this pain
I start the page again, stray the path again, on the road I go insane
Hide from myself, hide from everybody else as well
I hear the voices telling me that I must turn and walk away
Face the truth in the mirror, face the reflection of your fear
The mirror black, and all of life's dark clichés intact
I am powerless to fight…

Caught in the undertow, like an anchor pulling down
I am stuck in the mire, and I'm tired of the endless struggle to meet each
need
Conflicting interests and I'm alone to resolve the conflict
Find solutions to problems, the roots of which reach further than I am able
Demons rise to face me, eye to eye I am no match
How little I will fight if they want me

I've reached a point in my life where uncertainty rules the day
One moment to the next, I am here, I am there, really nowhere
In between the right and left, the right and wrong
I don't fit in or belong in this state of fallen grace
Face the truth in the mirror, face the reflection of your fear
The mirror black, and all of life's dark clichés intact
I am powerless to fight....

My Crucifixion

One of a few regrets, I face my mortality
Time spent in dissension, self imposed exile
I face my God, drop in prayer asking for reprieve
My penance; life, my sentence; life
In what else can I believe

Judge, jury, and executioner
Pontius Pilate at my crucifixion
I see things that most do not want to see
Blood on my hands
My own blood from my own crucifixion
Feeling things that most do not want to feel

I'm facing demons, living nightmares
As I am forced to look inside at the real me
Who I was, who I am, different yet the same
Fighting through the battles, torn and scarred
The only way to get over the shame

We all make mistakes, admitting it or not
I too was only created in an image
Falling short, falling hard, bottomless abyss
Truly sorry for the paths that I may have strayed
For the monsters I've created

Still I have become my judge, my jury, and my own
executioner
Pontius Pilate at my crucifixion
Seeing things that I don't want to see
Judge, jury, and executioner
Pontius Pilate at my crucifixion
Feeling things that I don't want to feel
Blood on my hands
My own blood from my own crucifixion
Believing things that I don't want to believe,
And all in the name of repentance...

Bless me father for I have sinned,
With my first breath of life I became tied to you
With a never-ending need for forgiveness…
Always sorry for the very way of the world

As if through death I could enact a change...

The Dark Half...

Demons trapped inside me
Released for the world to see
Awakened from their life-long slumber
At last they've been set free
My inner rage is the fire that fuels me
My anger seethes from every pore
No longer caged, my desire will rule me
A bloodlust to even the score

I am only half the monster being a man has made me
The other half is like a forgotten dream
Half the monster being a man has made me
The dark half that you now see…

I feel a rage like I've never felt before
To inflict pain in a way that cannot be forgotten
Years of suffering over, ended once and for all
Laid to rest with the bodies of those I'll leave for dead
Call my name and in my own grave you'll find me
Spark to flame I will rise as you are falling
I can't explain, not in words but in violent actions
Uncontrolled, exacting vengeance while slowly killing myself

I am only half the monster that being a man has made me
The other half is a forgotten dream
Half the monster being a man has made me
The dark half that you now see…

…In a reflection of the world around me,
I have become all that I have seen,
At times, that which I most despise…
The dark half that lives in me.

Roots of Evil...

We're walking on a tightrope
Above the gates of hell
There to harden our fall
At the bottom of the well
Souls that only suffer
They're calling out our names
We're walking into their arms
Directly into the flames
Unmoved by the heat
Marching blindly into defeat, we fall…

Roots of Evil, taking hold
Roots of Evil, reaching into our very souls
We're in their grip, we're under control

Of the root that which flowers
The gentle scent we hold so dear
From far below the spell was cast
And now the time draws near
You've been led on, I followed
Shall we meet the same fate
Will my path in time be hallowed
If I follow you through the gate
Unmoved by the heat
Marching blindly into defeat, we fall…

Roots of Evil, taking hold
Roots of Evil, reaching into our very souls
We're in their grip, we're under control

I punish myself for your crimes
And you watch but don't see my pain
I see myself as you time after time
Never once was anything gained
Still I'm following you
And the very root of your evil…

You've been led on, I followed
Shall we meet the same fate
Will my path in time be hallowed
If I follow you through the gate
Unmoved by the heat
Marching blindly into defeat, we fall…

My Epitaph...

As I look back and I see my life passed and I
Close my eyes so that I cannot see who is laughing last
I contemplate my choices, so misdirected
Can I straighten out the ship before it's too late??

Each and every day I think the thought
That this might be my last remembrance
And what do I bring to the empty table
For which a seat for me is always waiting
Every deed that is done has died before the day has gone
Every moment of peace conquered my inner war
Brought on from outside influence

I can't block out every negative
Cannot filter through the mire
I can't find hope with the positive
When it dies like my desire
The flames of life are flickering
The light it brought now fades
Contemplation of the end now
As I'm buried in the grave, My Epitaph

What carvings on my stone define me?
What actions or words left to inscribe
What memories have been left in my place?
And are they enough to keep me alive in your heart or mind

Another line, another page
All few and far between
Inspiration now found on an unknown stage
Because in this world I'll never be seen

I can't block every negative
Cannot filter through the mire
I can't find hope within the positive
When it dies like my desire
The flames of life are flickering
I'm a soul that won't be saved
Contemplation of the end now
As I'm buried in this grave, My Epitaph

What carvings on my stone define me?

Bleed for Me...

I speak in anger
Spewing rage with each new breath
The fire burns within me; exacting fight
And I know the duel is to the death

No right or wrong
I wreak my vengeance
I stand alone, strength without numbers
A leader not a follower;
Understand this…

I will take all that I need
Even as I sit and watch you bleed
Bleed; bleed for me
Bleed for my amusement
Because you are in the way of what I need, bleed

I look your way
Eyes burning through your every move
I watch your steps
Are you watching out for yourself?
All I can say is that you had better tread lightly
Because in my world, you are not standing on solid ground
It's time to meet the maker
The payment long overdue is now being collected…

I will take all that I need even as I sit and watch you bleed
Bleed, Bleed, but not for me
But for all of the lines you have crossed without reason

Drowning Out The Truth

You say you've made a friend in the bottle
In the number one solution
You're getting loose watching drop after drop
Straighten all the confusion
You want to keep the party rolling on
Refusing to face the facts
The way you live each day, day in and out
The story can end so sad

You've got to see the light
Through the night; black night
Don't waste your youth
Drowning out the truth

What you used to understand without question
You now admit with hesitation
As if in your mind you're not sure
And the cause, only frustration
I want to know that you can see through the haze
But at times it seems as thick as mud
You're searching for all the answers
But you're losing hold of what was

...I know all about feeling good
So many days I've felt that way
But it's not an escape, just a delay in the game
Because when it's over everything is the same....

You've got to see the light
Through the night; black night
Don't waste your youth
Drowning out the truth

Life, my friend, right now to you is such a joke
But as a friend I can see your pain
I know your eyes, no you can't disguise
Bloodshot lines spell out your shame

You've got to see the light
Through the night; black night
Don't waste your youth
Drowning out the truth

Desolate...

Wandering aimless
Through twilight city streets at night
Invisible to the outside world
Nothing really right
Looking, longing, wondering when I will see
That always bright, reflective light
The end of the tunnel

Another night of sorrows
Drown in open bottles
Fluid for the times of your life
And remedy for the tears we've shed
But in the end you'll be blinded
By broken seal, on broken bottle
You will stay on the dark side of the tunnel
Never see light

Living in darkness for years of my life
I'll continue to strive while I'm still alive
But not by my choice…
Guardian angel chose me to live this life
Desolate life, I am unsure how long I can live it

In The Name of the Father...

Everyone gets the chance to believe in their God
At least once in our lives we all look to him for strength
Everyone has the opportunity to engage in his faith
Faith that can move the mountains
For the souls who can't be saved by themselves

There's a solemn voice that cried to me one day
A voice within myself that is whispering again
In the name of the Father are the words I am trying to say
In the name of the Father, I pray…

As one in congregation, all gathering in mass
Asking for forgiveness and for all suffering to pass
For those who have been before and for those still to come
One voice is rising up in anticipation of salvation

There's a solemn voice that cried to me one day
A voice within myself that is whispering again
In the name of the Father are the words I am trying to say
And in the name of the Father, I pray…

Hope is for the hopeless ones and faith for the faithless
Redemption waits for everyone
As one we're no longer faceless…

As one in congregation gathering in mass
Asking for forgiveness and for all suffering to pass
For those who have been before and for those still to come
One voice is rising up in anticipation of salvation

…In the name of the Father are the words I am trying to say
And in the name of the Father, we pray…

Baptism in Fire...

I've seen the worst
Been both blessed and cursed
Just another day in the life
For this passenger of time
I speak in riddle
At times end up in rhyme
There are days that I walk
And days that I run away from the world
Because I do not like what I'm seeing

The dreams I've seen are passing away
As strength falls prey to weakness
All tangled in the fray
Pulled under by the current
Its unrelenting torrent
Of twisted misunderstood emotions
That play themselves out on my world

Guided by a certain bleakness
A feeling so forlorn
Yet beneath its numbing veil
There's a sense of comfort and warmth
Over and over I find myself returning
For the pleasure of the pain
Salt in the wound won't stop the burning
It's only fuel for the flame

And it's the Father, the Son,
And the Holy Ghost that I thank
For my Baptism in Fire…

Dead of Night...

I am talking to myself in the dead of night
Waiting for responses from my shadow
Distant echoes ringing through my brain
Bring me to rise and gaze outside my window

I look for answers, resume the endless search
But I lurch ahead as slow as can be
Unable to grasp and understand the feelings
That only I must be able to see or to feel

I feign loneliness just to get away
To reach a point that seems solid and seems real
So I can understand in my heart and in my head deeply
That you can possibly feel all of the things I feel

Call me a sensitive little monster
Sweet talk me back into your charm
But I am not half the monster that being a man has made me
I can keep us safe from harm…

But I am talking to myself in the dead of night
Crying out to shadow reflected in soft light
Black to gray to white is the general progression
What else to live for, why else to fight!!
In the Dead of Night…

Torment...

I lie awake at night and I can't fall asleep
Recounting every single detail
Of my life that's passed and surely can't be lived again
Mistakes I've made and never learned from

I stare in darkness at the pictures on the wall
Waiting for their stories to unfold before me
But I don't see a thing, nor to hear a sound
Only the gears in my mind that keep turning

I watch the clock each night and track the time
As it changes and nothing within me moves
Dreamless again the ceiling always looks the same
And death, in my mind can't be much worse

I need to change the way that I see the world
Or turning my back should I walk away
Too many people in life that I simply cannot face
With motives of self and no one else's needs

I find again that the night is not a friend
But a wolf in sheepskin, staring, lurking
Waiting for the moment when it may pounce and feed
On every weakness that lives and breathes in me

Heart and soul and in every breath I take
I feel the torment tearing through me
And I can't free myself from the awful truths
As I am lying here waiting for the death of me...

Fit of Rage...

Can't control your conviction
Over the exact order of things
Won't second guess your emotion
To sacrifice your needs
But then the line is strayed
Your uncharted course
Time after time you scream out
In a fit of rage…
Oh, Oh, Oh, in a fit of rage…

It all seems so simple
To see things the right way
If we're open to compromise
And mean the things we say
And it seems ridiculous
That certain things must happen
I've had it up to here and I'll scream out
In a fit of rage…
Oh, Oh, Oh, in a fit of rage…

…I try to talk myself into believing how things have to be
Attain the unattainable, constantly achieve
Pushing to be as one, unlike any other…
I've got to scream out, in a fit of rage

My eyes are deceiving me, a blind man in a cave
Feeling for an answer, eternal freedom for a slave
Years, I said years of sacrifice and self-inflicted pain
Now, before my eyes a lifetime
It is my hope all was not in vain…
Still time and again I'll scream out
In a fit of rage…

Shed My Skin...

Seething beneath the surface
Eruption is imminent
Not a question of if, but when
And the time is drawing near…

Frustration building on the inside
Dissension growing all around
Years of turmoil finally boiling over
Leaving nothing unscathed in its wake

The time has come to shed the skin that has contained me
Revealing to the world, the real me
The concealed me…
And some may not like what they see
My demise may result from my actions
And my words may seal my fate
Carved in stone on the walls
That I intend to bring down around me

…. Unfortunate by true, are the feelings
That lie within me
Chains that have forever held me bound
But now my strength is growing and my
Rage to overcome is building
And the price will be paid one thousand times over
By everyone in my path….

The time has come to shed the skin that has contained me
….Revealing to the world, the real me
The concealed me……
And some may not like who it is and what it is they see

The End of the Line...

I can't let anyone into my world now
As the utter decay of my spirit spreads
I crawl alone into the abyss of my own making
Left to ponder the remainder of my existence

What is left for me to prove, how much left to lose
When all that I may have needed is already gone
And the family that I thought I knew, I have left behind
And those closest to me
Don't even know who I am…
As I am left to ask, do I?

What I stood for, where I stand, foundations have crumbled,
And I am tumbling down
The eternal fall, into the never-ending void
That is the reality of this, my world now

Thankless world that we love and grieve in
Wretched world that I live and breathe in
Unforgiving world that we bleed and die in
And for nothing more than one day of mourning
Nothing more than memories and words
At the end of the line…

Worlds Apart...

The words are in my head but I don't know what to say
And I don't know where to start; we're worlds apart…

So many years of love between us
So many days of joy we've shared
So many countless nights of passion
And now we feel the wear and tear
Can't see through the wall between us
Can't live through the endless fight
Can't survive the pain or pressure
Close our eyes to the blinding light

The words are in my head but still I don't know what to say
And I don't know where to start; because we're worlds apart…

Seen through your eyes or through mine
I believe the picture looks the same
The truth is all wrapped up in lies
And neither of us can hide the shame
Not one of us better than the other
We both can read between the lines
With each passing day it grows much clearer
We both have seen the warning signs

The words are all within my head but some things I just won't say
And I don't know where to start; we are worlds apart…

Another night of useless struggle
As you now dream asleep at rest
And tomorrow come the morning
I will arise to another breath
And as another day of endless longing
Begins to come alive in me
Still another part now weeping
Will fail to open its eyes and see

The words are all within my head but I don't know what to say
And I don't know where to start; we are worlds apart…

Verge of Collapse...

I look around me at friends and enemies
Unable to really tell who is who
A handshake with one hand and a backstab with the other
Depending on which will suit their needs

I fall prey to the theory that all men are good
A fool in the darkness is what I've become
A change in the making for better or for worse
I will stand alone apart from the others
As much as I've done for the people I know
No thought of myself getting anything in return
The benefit of others was my only cause
Now for the benefit of myself and only those I love

I have been living on the verge of collapse
Carrying the weight of my world
Bend till I break on the verge of collapse
Carrying the weight of the world…

Wolves in sheep skin that I have let in
In the den of the devil I now see deep within
Beneath the surface I see the true face
Of the demon inside that must be erased
So hard to be truthful yet so easy to lie
So hard to tell by the look in their eyes
Time is the keeper that will set all truths free
And somewhere in time they will have to face me

I have been living on the verge of collapse
Carrying the weight of my world
Bend till I break on the verge of collapse
Carrying the weight of the world…

Sins of the past always come back to haunt me
Though I've forgiven anyone against me
In my heart I have changed for the better I think
And my soul I thought cleansed is still on the brink
Pray to my God for an end to this dream
More of a nightmare than I could believe
To do right, to work hard, and at the end of the day
Be at peace with myself, again in silence I pray…

I have been living on the verge of collapse…

Tonight...

It seems we can talk for hours
And never find a solution
It's so late, but I'm wide awake
Within my mind a revolution
In the middle with no way out
Only time tells the story
I am part of the cast, but can I last
Will I live to share the glory?

Tonight, the world ceases to turn
Tonight, I see how much I must learn
Tonight, I'm facing reality
Tonight, there's nothing to set me free

Its times like these I must survive
Make it through the night
Watch for the sun, it's sure to come
To turn things around and make them right
The birds have started singing
A sign morning is on the way
I still need to dream
Or will I wake with a scream on the new day

Tonight, the world ceases to turn
Tonight, I see how much I must learn
Tonight, I'm facing reality
Tonight, there's nothing to set me free

I've seen the top of the world
And it's higher up than I've ever been
But I've been through the longest, darkest nights
Caught in a web of sin
Now I'm somewhere in between
I reach for the top but I'm pulled back down
I don't believe some of the things I've seen
I don't know if tomorrow will ever come around

For right now, I'm frightened
Someone show me how
To fight off the pain
That runs through my brain tonight...

For The Living... (Already Dead)

As creativity wanes, my spirit, it also fades ......

No room left for living
But I am far too young to die
No energy left for giving
Because my return are the tears I cry
Whispers are my voice unheard
Fainter breaths you'll never breathe
And the life that I am living
Still won't allow me to see

The meanings that elude me
Are the answers I seek to find?
The dreams that die for me each day
Remind me of my fleeting time here
Can't overcome the weather
Heavy clouds obstruct my view
Follow my heart or follow my head
Neither is sure of what to do anymore

I live my life for the living
For I am already dead
No return for all the giving
In the end it is as I said,
Already dead

...I try to imagine what it must be like to live
Try to remember if I ever really did
The wasted years that got me through
The darkest fears I've ever known
Haven't benefited me in any way
And as my unspoken words have yet to reveal
I'm like a book that has never been opened...

So I live my life for the living
Because I am already dead
The lesson I learned is the one that I'm giving
Because in the end it is as I said, I'm already dead

Enslaved

Writing,
And fighting for freedom
For I am bound to the Beast in chains…

The dungeon master is calling
And the shackled prisoner falling
On his knees, He cries
He pleas, for mercy on his very soul

Believe his days are passing him by
He believes he'll never last, but why
All around the sound of death calls
Echoing madly off of the walls

The cell is cold like life gone by
The rats, they gaze into his eyes
He dreams of days of sunlit mornings
But only night will visualize

Enslaved in a kingdom of repression
Where the torture of man is their obsession
And when you lie at rest near death
They cut your chains and set you free

You can express not the slightest emotion
You can be crushed down in one motion
Flesh and bone, not a trace of spirit
Enslaved in this realm, forevermore

The Only One...

The print is bold and the thoughts I long to share
Can shatter our far reaching foundation
Everything is coming back at me
And I'm trying hard to find some relation to this
moment in my life
Why now do you come to pass?
Choose now to wage your war
Am I just another of life's victims
That happened to have the mark upon my door?

Once the second son, now the only one
The darkened hand reaches out to pull me through
Once the second son, now the only one
And there is only one thing I can do…..
Follow you through to the other side

Out of the light left in my world
And into the dark that is your light
Where once I could see
Now I am blind to purpose and reason
And the bleakness of your promise
Finally engulfs me and traps me in…..
In what seems like doom forever
There is no blue behind the gray
No distant hope or penance left to pray
That in this life I might be saved

Once the second son, now the only one
The darkened hand reaches out to pull me through
Once the second son, now the only one
With only one thing left to do, follow you through
to the other side…..
The dark side of my imagination

Shadow Land...

Walking and talking
On through a silver forest
Enchanted birds either sing
Or give up their wings
As the magician controls all things
Time stands still if that is his will
He has ways of making you believe

He's a magic man, lives in magic land
And I have seen in disbelief his tricks
Is he more than a magic man
In what now seems a foreign land
Heaven, Hell, and Earth are at his command

The powers that be
Altering images of time and space
Defying nature's laws to cover up all of the flaws
His realm of magic the only cause
Lost in a scheme that's just a deadly dream
With the strength to conquer anyone

Walking and talking
On through a silver forest
The sun is rising, the shadows playing
Games of time whose secrets are undiscovered
Plain and simply, days without numbers
Time will stand still if that's his will
He has ways of making us believe…

He is a magic man
Lives in a magic land,
Shadow Land…

Part of Me... (Passion)

Nowhere left to go
But to return home
Safely locked away
For the remainder of my life
And in my passing what part of me remains
What part of me will be retained
Or detained at the gate
As I pass into my next life

And tell me, who's to say
Who is to say what awaits each of us
On the other side…

Eternal life, eternal night
The light of day or
The dead of night
What I saw, what you see
Who is to say what part of me
will be left behind
Or at very least to carry on…

Mortality was not for me
In order to travel beyond this realm
I've had to step outside my shell
To walk unhindered to my next destination
I journey, traveling
Beyond the center, earth
Far removed from my body,
My spirit soars…

But what part of me remains
My suffering could not have been in vain
For the lesson we all must learn
Is the one alone I'll die for

The part of me that sees beyond belief
That believes beyond what I see
My all consuming passion...

On the Wagon...

I'm on the wagon
Out to slay the dragon
His breath of fire always one step behind
I'm on the wagon
Out to slay the dragon
With my only weapon
The power stored within my mind…

Cleaning up the act
Facing all the facts
When you were burning you know you couldn't see
Removing the blindfold
The truth is seen and told
Now you're cooling down and fighting to be free

You've got to get away
Find someplace to stay
Immune to temptation as it looks for you
Start it once again
The beginning of the end
You've failed to see all that it has yet to do

I'm on the wagon, out to slay the dragon
His breath of fire always one step behind
On the wagon, out to slay the dragon
With my only weapon
The power stored within my mind…

Look straight into the mirror
How do things appear?
Can you make out through the haze, the bloodshot eyes
Remember the times you said, that's it?
All those times you'd never quit
Can you, yourself, live with all of the lies?

I am on the wagon, out to slay the dragon
With his breath of fire always one step behind...

Dead in the Water...

There is a rope around my neck
About where the dead bird will be hung
And the weight upon my chest
Leaves no air left in my lungs
Impossible to breathe,
Impossible to see beyond today
And tomorrow is the beginning of another end again…

I find myself standing still
Dead in the water, unable to move
I see myself drifting, fading away
Nothing at all left to lose; I am dead in the water

In defeat I let the waves engulf and take me in
Drowning in the depths only despair can bring
Reaching out for faith to finally cleanse the sin
In and out of hope, sorrow worn like a ring
Again the weight is upon me
Again, impossible to breathe
And beyond today there is nothing
Perhaps tomorrow we'll see the change

I find myself standing still
I am dead in the water,
I see myself drifting, fading away
Nothing at all left to lose; dead in the water

My Failure...

And all of the hopes that I held so high
Have returned again to echo my failure...

I'm looking back into my youth through fading pictures that I see
I wonder if I'll find the truth, is it too late to be set free
I feel my age has finally crept upon a grim reality
Long ago my life was changed and the reflections aren't of me

No lessons learned through pages turned or tablets carved in stone
Past mistakes repeat themselves and I'm left standing here alone
...And all of the hopes that I held so high
Have returned again to echo my failures
Echo my failure...

Searching inside to find strength through faith for the chance rise again
I pray for a new beginning as I know I have reached an end
One last wish from the bottom of the well and time can only tell
If facing all these truths can finally break the lifelong spell

No lessons learned through pages turned or tablets carved in stone
Stolen breaths I can never breathe and I'm left standing here alone
...And all of the hope that I held so high
Have returned again to echo my failures
Echo my failure...

Answers...(In Vain)

I cut my wrist in anger
I watch my world fade
To death I'm not a stranger
It was I that wielded its blade
A victim of my silence
That screamed out in my head
Self-Inflicted violence
Watch, as my life pours out in red

There are no easy answers, why try to explain
The one and only answer
Is for the life that was lived out in vain
A life that was lived out in vain...

You'll see my spirit soaring
Freed from its earthly bond
Factions of good and evil warring
Over the soul they both have found
Will I ascend to heaven?
Or will I burn in hell
Is there life after my death?
Or is six feet deep the bottom of the well
From where I'm at it's hard to tell...

I cross my hands in prayer
Was it meant to end this way?
I cut my wrist in anger
And now I watch as my life fades
A victim of this violence
In self-inflicted rage
Forever free of the screaming silence
My words in blood no longer stain the page

There are no easy answers, why try to explain
The one and only answer
Is for the life that was lived out in vain
A life lived out in vain…

…Will I ascend to heaven?
Or will I burn in hell
Is there life after my death?
Or is six feet deep the bottom of the well
From where I'm at it's hard to tell…

Tragic...

We mourn your loss we've lost your love
A star so bright that now shines above us
No earthly glow remains yet still we know
You'll follow with us wherever we go

Behind your smile and the gleam in your eye
How could we know all you felt inside
The inner pain and emptiness we now feel
There is no escaping that which is real

We watched as you grew from child to man
Watched as your father and mother let go of your hand
We watched as you conquered those childhood fears
Watched as your focus became crystal clear

Your family and friends could see it in your eyes
How you lived everyday and how you loved your life
So many were touched by the love in your heart
And now we carry that with us though we're torn apart

It's tragic to think, it's tragic to feel
Still so hard to believe any of this is real
The words that I've found within me can barely explain
The feelings I have for your family, our family in pain...

The Other Side...

A part of my life will be coming to an end
Whether a chapter or a verse
Either for the better or for the worse
It's really hard to say in the state I'm in
I'm squeezing through this tunnel
And though I'm sure I see a light
I realize each day is so full of cliché
I'm unsure of what awaits me …
On the other side

I try to piece together all of the parts
That broke free in the wreckage
What resemblance does this have of me
The man that I thought I once was?
Overcome the heavy rain
To be confronted by the darkest day
Is there a way for me to erase the stain
Or a better way for me to pray…

I'm squeezing through this tunnel
And though I'm sure I see a light
Every day is another cliché
And I'm unsure of what awaits me…, on the other side

The Setting Sun ...

I look out over the horizon at what has past
The shadows cast upon my life
And the light of the sun that I no longer see
I once felt its warmth, once felt no shroud
could block its rays
Now as I enter a new stage in my life, the dusk
And not the dawn will guide me

Weary of the world, of the hectic pace of life
I'm forced to keep
The energy of youth has faded and the uphill climb
Is far too steep
A victim of the chaos, every day has placed
upon me
A victim of the belief that there is no tomorrow
Waiting beyond today

I awake each day not wanting the night to end
I lay down to sleep each day not wanting the night to begin
Not near enough to the start yet to far from the finish
Somewhere, here in the middle of my life
Purpose is the forgotten cause

I lack the sleep to rest in peace, lack the peace
to sleep at rest
Unable to begin again and somehow unable to change
Caught in this state, void of all understanding
Unable to see beyond the darkness
That seems to have fallen again
With the setting of the sun…

Visionary...

A visionary in the darkness
Who can't see a thing
Longing for an intense light
And the joy it would bring
From the past, lost horizons
Are they lost for good
For one more chance he holds on
Longer maybe than anyone could

In my mind I see a way, a day
A time to rejoice
I see the weak, a chance to speak
All raising up their voices
In my mind I see the surface
And straight through to the depths
I'm looking for hearts broken apart
Anyone longing for a saving breath

A visionary in the darkness
A shroud cast by his surrounds
Longing for an intense light
And a love that has no bounds
A believer whose faith is his strength
The endless reaches of his might
Surviving in the darkness
In a world of near endless night

So Much to Live For...

Night has fallen on us again
The light of the sun has faded for the stars
Against the dark sky
The moon now in its glory
Reflecting through the trees
And every picture tells a story
Depending on who sees

I gaze into infinity
Never reaching an end on the horizon
What goes around will come around
We carry the circle with us through time

Never knowing where to start or to finish
I carry on getting lost in the rhyme
Waiting for the idea to grow or diminish
I'm so in love with life
So deeply in love with you, Adrianne

Sometimes I'm lost, not knowing what to do
Because I want so much for us that up until now
I wasn't sure we could have
But now, after fulfilling this sacrifice to each other
I know, I truly believe
Everything that seemed out of reach is now within our grasp

You; Adrianne are my strength when I'm weak
And I yours…
You are my anchor when I need stability
And I yours…
You; above all are my life and my love
And with you I can finally begin to live this dream
A dream that begins and ends with you by my side
And I by yours...

Now we can truly live, to make the most of life
The most of ourselves, for each other and our future
That on this night looks so bright and full of promise
Like the moon this night reflecting on the water
My eyes are focused on us, on our tomorrow
There is so much to live for…

New Lease on Life...

I've got to prove it to myself
And not to anybody else
I've got a new lease on life
Sharper than a razor or any knife

I'm in search of better things
Not the fame and fortune they might bring
If I want to live, I've got to give
Push myself a little harder
Reach new peaks that hide
I'll seek them

Surge ahead, run a big risk
There must be more to life than this
Laying around, lost not found
Dusk till dawn without ambition
Breaking loose and free
Eluding the noose again

I'll have to change my ways but I'll remain the same
I have dreams like you but they won't die, they'll come true someway
More of this and less of that, but I won't refuse a good excuse
To through it all away…

If I want to live, I've got to give
Push myself a little harder
Reach new peaks that hide, I'll seek them

I'll break my neck, keep working hard
It's better to feast than it is to starve
Do my best to pass every test
In search of better things, like
Reaching new peaks that hide,
I'll seek them…

Proving it to myself
And not to anybody else
I've got a new lease on life
Sharper than a razor or any knife

Hold You...

I've got so much on my mind
I'm thinking about you
So many empty feelings from the past
That are no longer true
You mean so much to me
You are filling up my time
And in my one track mind
You are the only one I see

Just being near you is enough for me to feel complete,
Just to have you as a thought within my mind…
You've become again
A daily reminder of what really matters
And deep in my heart I hold you…

How often I talk about you
To myself or to someone else
So many emotions spilling over themselves
From my heart to yours
I have got to find a way
To tell you how I'm feeling
Before you're gone
Before I run away from my feelings

Just being near you is enough for me to feel complete,
Just to have you as a thought within my mind…
You've become again
A daily reminder of what really matters
And deep in my heart I hold you…

Kill For You...

Words like poison arrows
That are piercing right through you
Intending to break your spirit
And drain the lifeblood right from you
In your mind you see the truth but
In your heart you've lost the will
But in my mind I feel a rage come alive
And in my heart I know I will, I would

Kill for you, crush the life from within
Kill for you, without regard for the sin
Kill for you, put an end to a physical life, and I will
Die for you, if it would help you through this night

Heartless in his verbal attack
Just because he thinks he can
With no respect for a woman, or self
The sign of a weakened man
Believe in yourself, you are so much better than this
And believe in me, as hard as that may sometimes seem to be

I would kill for you, crush the life from within
Kill for you, without regard for the sin
Kill for you, put an end to a physical life, I will
Die for you, if it would help you through this night

…a reminder will be sent his way
So he knows everyone will know…
And his own words will be the death of him
When no one looks at him the same again
"Ungrateful son of a bitch,
What a waste you are,
Just another pile of mankind's shit
is exactly what you are"

I would kill for you, I would die for you…
Just to help you make it through this night

Parallels... (Somehow)

The more that time passes
The more I understand
Why you would reach your hand out to the other side
The world all around you
That you never felt like a part of
Continued to fool you and fail you until you could finally take no more

Parallel lives in a perpendicular world
You and I may share the same path
And our father, bless his soul
Somehow may have paved the road we travel…

A difficult decision you made
To fade into the oblivion of eternal of eternal sleep
And day by day you inched one step closer
Through the varying depths of pain
Finally to reach the ultimate peace

Parallel lives in a perpendicular world
You and I may share the same path
And our father, bless his soul
Somehow may have paved the road we travel…

…No denying the inevitable,
No fighting the curse of the damned
Somehow lost, somehow forgotten souls
Left behind in the madness…

Parallel lives in a perpendicular world
You and I may share the same path
And our father, bless his soul
Somehow may have paved the road we travel…You and I my brother, you and I…

Hunger...

From out of this world comes a hell we call life
They call life a gift from God above, but what about me
What about the love in my stone cold heart
Lying dormant now for years…

A simple man making futile attempts at reason
Finding excuses for his actions
But all he asks is satisfaction
For the hungers in his heart

In legend sleeping beauty dies
Only to be awakened by the kiss of love
In her place now, I lay on pyre
Awaiting love as spiritual fire
To bring me new life after emotional death…

A simple man making futile attempts at reason
Finding excuses for his actions
But all he asks is satisfaction
For the hungers in his heart

Riding into sunsets
Long shadows fall behind you
Happily ever after only happens
In the tales we read, in the dreams we weave
What matters most is not our inner happiness
But those things so immaterial…

A simple man making futile attempts at reason
Finding excuses for his actions
But all he asks is satisfaction
For the hungers in his heart

Endurance...

Clutching hard at my pillow, why can't I let it go
I'm talking to myself alone and wonder it is I know
I'll sit and torment myself, I do it without any help
Not from you, not from anyone, because I can fire my own gun

You know I can really put the pressure on, really lay myself to rest
And I wonder if I have the endurance
To rise to the occasion, to pass each and every test…

But do I come out in the end ahead
Will anything I've ever said be remembered
One single word begins a verse for the day
And the last line signals the end of the page

The saga has to be continued
If only for the sake of pushing on
The picture you paint will be a part of the view
The picture you paint for those surrounding you

You know I can really put the pressure on, really lay myself to rest
And I wonder if I have the endurance
To rise to the occasion, to pass each and every test…

Reaching down into yourself
You'll find all it is you'll need
Sometimes a wish in the last drop of the well
Will be the one which sows the seed

...It's a struggle to endure, a fight to stay alive
But there really isn't any other choice
...So many distractions to stifle ones drive
But there really isn't any other choice; Endure

Reaching down into yourself
You'll find all it is you'll need
Sometimes a wish in the last drop of the well
Will be the one which sows the seed...

I'm the One...

Times have changed; I can barely find the words
No longer rhyming anymore
It seems my imagination is not as bright as it used to be
I cannot find the magic door
But I've since read something, someone said so long ago
The written word spoken with conviction
It's coming back at me, all at once it's rushing by
And I breathe a sigh, the pain is fading

I'm thinking back…
Memory banks have served good interest income
I run the risk again of never knowing if I'll come back again
But it's a risk I love to run; it's only a game of one on one
…And I'm the one

Yes, I'm reaching out; I may be an endangered specie
I'm not sure if I understand what it means
But can you appreciate that I'm following my instincts
So much more can be read if you look in between
Is there a lesson to learn in speaking my mind
It's fact, far from fiction giving sight to the blind
If I print can you read through a cluster of letters
That through hope and faith will hard times turn better

I'm thinking back…
Memory banks have served good interest income
I run the risk again of never knowing if I'll come back again
But it's a risk I love to run; it's only a game of one on one
…And I'm the one

...So am I the one to tell you and I the one to set the scene
How many of you will know what I mean?

I'm think back...
Memory banks have served good interest income
I run the risk again of never knowing if I'll come back again
But it's a risk I love to run; it's only a game of one on one
...And I'm the one

Shades to Red...

Sitting, gazing through the window
Wondering where you are
I can't stop watching through the pane
At every passing car
Each footstep or each whisper
Brings me to my feet
I rise to look outside for you
And then I fall back in my seat

...Tell me honey, where are you
As the evening sky shades to red
Walking. talking in the moonlight
An image clouds my head
Is it fear that makes me feel this way?
As the evening sky shades to red...

I know that I am losing you
You're nowhere to be found
I'm stubborn but I'm foolish too
To think you'll stick around
It's hard to put our lives together
It's as if we were bound to break
We wonder why, we say whatever
Never thinking of what's at stake

...Tell me honey, where are you
When the evening sky shades to red
Walking, talking in the moonlight
An image clouds my head
Is it fear that makes me feel this way?
As the evening sky shades to red...

I can't believe the things I'm thinking
They are tearing me apart
The lone survivor is finally sinking
The coldness filled my heart
Like lead I'm falling to the bottom
No longer reaching for the top
Once past the point of no return
There is no real reason to stop

…So tell me honey, where are you, when the evening sky shades to red
Walking and talking in the moonlight, an image clouds my head
Is it fear that makes me feel this way, as the evening sky shades to red…?

Summer Days...

These summer days
Have their crazy ways
Of driving me insane
These summer days
Have their crazy ways
Of making me do things that I can't explain...

Yes, there is a feeling in the air
Like magic it comes out of nowhere
It gives me something to believe in
When my spirit is lost in the wind
It approaches my heavy heart only to lighten my load
To deal me some fresh cards just as I was about to fold

You know, these summer days
Have their crazy ways
Of turning me around
In some strange way
These crazy summer days
Will pick you up when you are really down...

I am gazing into cloudless sky
Infinite blue is all that meets my eye
But in my mind the echoes linger on
Unanswered questions with each new dawn
But something in the air gives me the feeling
That I can achieve anything I want to if I don't give in

These summer days
Have their crazy ways
Of clearing up the view
Yes, in some strange way
These crazy summer days
Make me feel like there is nothing that I can't do…

Gazing into cloudless sky
Infinite blue is all that meets my eye…

Passion Play...

Singing praises of my idols
For whatever the reasons be
You can draw your own conclusions
Or you can take a ride, just a little ride with me

Magic and mystery in pursuit
The madness draws me near
Living a dream state, bordering on nightmare
Still it is only God that I fear

Putting together shattered pieces
Like bodies on a battlefield
Uncovering bits and pieces of our pasts
Bitter seeds producing bitter yields

So tell me, what is there to lose
Following me on a journey
Realism has no meaning
And I can take you wherever you choose to be

Sail ships through misty ocean
Current pulls astray
Tossing and turning onto the rocks
Reefs of yesterday
Climbing highest mountain
Caught in this passion play
A drink from the mythical fountain
And our guide shall lead the way
Shall we…
Take me away, on a passion play…

Two In One...

I talk about the distant past as if it were yesterday
I talk about tomorrow as if it will never come
I think aloud, but I am lost in the crowd
I'm standing still, but I want so much to run

I tell myself one thing and mean entirely something else
I hide from my shadow because it's more real than me
And all of the words in the world cannot change the fact
That inside and out I have got two identities

…I am two in one, multiple personality
Two in one, one in chains and the other free
And there times when I can't separate one from the other
Times when the couch and the chair look the same
And the real game is finding out what kind of man I am…
Two in one

I say to myself that I'm no different than the rest
But when I look in the mirror what do I see
A hard working man that wants nothing but the best
All draped in chains that I cannot shake free

You may think you know me, but I know better
You may believe there are many like me
But no one in this world feels my feelings
Fathomless depths not many dare tread

...I am two in one, multiple personality
Two in one, one in chains and the other free
And there are times when I can't separate one from the other
Times when the couch and the chair look the same
And the real game is finding out what kind of man I am...
Two in one

What you see is only a fraction of the whole...
I am two in one, one in chains and the other free...
Two in one

Printed in the United States
By Bookmasters